SUPER SIMPLE
SCIENCE AT WORK

SUPER SIMPLE
EXPERIMENTS
WITH
ELEMENTS

FUN AND INNOVATIVE SCIENCE PROJECTS

PAIGE V. POLINSKY

CONSULTING EDITOR, DIANE CRAIG, M.A./READING SPECIALIST

Super Sandcastle

An Imprint of Abdo Publishing
abdopublishing.com

abdopublishing.com

Published by Abdo Publishing, a division of ABDO, PO Box 398166, Minneapolis, Minnesota 55439. Copyright © 2017 by Abdo Consulting Group, Inc. International copyrights reserved in all countries. No part of this book may be reproduced in any form without written permission from the publisher. Super SandCastle™ is a trademark and logo of Abdo Publishing.

Printed in the United States of America, North Mankato, Minnesota
062016
092016

 THIS BOOK CONTAINS RECYCLED MATERIALS

Editor: Liz Salzmann
Content Developer: Nancy Tuminelly
Cover and Interior Design and Production: Mighty Media, Inc.
Photo Credits: Mighty Media, Inc.; Shutterstock

The following manufacturers/names appearing in this book are trademarks: Arm & Hammer®, Duracell®, Gedney®, Morton®, Pyrex®, Total®, Total Home®, Up & Up™

Library of Congress Cataloging-in-Publication Data

Names: Polinsky, Paige V., author.
Title: Super simple experiments with elements : fun and innovative science projects / Paige V. Polinsky ; consulting editor, Diane Craig, M.A./reading specialist.
Description: Minneapolis, Minnesota : Abdo Publishing, [2017] | | Series: Super simple science at work
Identifiers: LCCN 2016006220 (print) | LCCN 2016013048 (ebook) | ISBN 9781680781687 (print) | ISBN 9781680776119 (ebook)
Subjects: LCSH: Chemical elements--Juvenile literature. | Science--Experiments--Juvenile literature. | Science projects—Juvenile literature.
Classification: LCC QD466 .P568 2016 (print) | LCC QD466 (ebook) | DDC 507.8--dc23
LC record available at http://lccn.loc.gov/2016006220

Super SandCastle™ books are created by a team of professional educators, reading specialists, and content developers around five essential components—phonemic awareness, phonics, vocabulary, text comprehension, and fluency—to assist young readers as they develop reading skills and strategies and increase their general knowledge. All books are written, reviewed, and leveled for guided reading and early reading intervention programs for use in shared, guided, and independent reading and writing activities to support a balanced approach to literacy instruction.

To Adult Helpers

The projects in this title are fun and simple. There are just a few things to remember to keep kids safe. Some projects require the use of sharp or hot objects. Also, kids may be using messy materials such as glue or paint. Make sure they protect their clothes and work surfaces. Review the projects before starting, and be ready to assist when necessary.

....

KEY SYMBOL

Watch for this warning symbol in this book. Here is what it means.

 SHARP!
You will be working with a sharp object. Get help!

CONTENTS

ELEMENTS
AT WORK

Elements are everywhere! We breathe in oxygen from the air. We drink hydrogen in water. We eat iron in cereal. And our bodies are made up of elements!

An element is made of one type of atom. Everything is made of atoms. An atom is made of electrons, neutrons, and protons.

Atoms can bond with each other. Bonded atoms are called **molecules**.

HYDROGEN IN WATER

IRON IN CEREAL

118 ELEMENTS

Today scientists know of 118 elements. Each atom has a certain number of protons. The number of protons is called an atomic number. Every element has a different atomic number. The atomic number is how elements are identified.

Elements are organized into the periodic table in the order of their atomic numbers. Each element is represented by a **symbol**. The symbol can be one, two, or three letters. The periodic table also shows each element's atomic number.

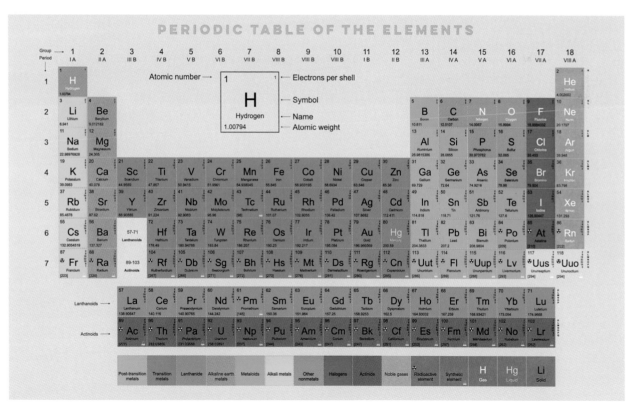

COMPOUNDS

Pure elements are made of one kind of atom. But elements can bond with other elements. This creates compound **molecules**. Water is a compound. Oxygen and hydrogen atoms bond to form water molecules.

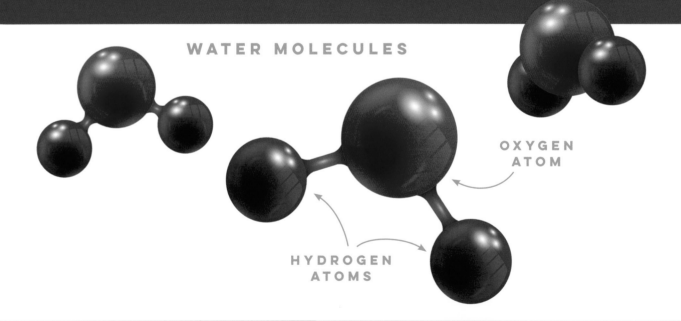

WATER MOLECULES

OXYGEN ATOM

HYDROGEN ATOMS

Sugar is a compound of carbon, hydrogen, and oxygen. So is **starch**, such as the starch in potatoes! The difference between starch and sugar is the number of each type of atom in the **molecules**.

SUGAR CUBES

POTATOES

REACTIONS

A chemical **reaction** is when two or more molecules interact. This causes the molecules to change. Bonds between atoms break or form to create new molecules. An example of a chemical reaction is rusting steel. Steel has iron in it. The iron molecules bond with oxygen molecules in the air. Water helps the bonds form. This reaction makes iron oxide, the chemical name for rust.

WORK LIKE
A SCIENTIST

You've learned about elements. Now you're ready to experiment! Scientists have a special way of working. It is called the Scientific Method. Follow the steps to work like a scientist. It's super simple!

THE SCIENTIFIC METHOD

Have a notebook and pencil handy. Scientists write down everything that happens in their experiments. They also write down their thoughts and ideas.

1. QUESTION

What question are you trying to answer? Write down your question. Then do some **research** to find out more about it.

2. GUESS

Try to guess the answer to your question. Write down your guess.

MARIE CURIE

Marie Curie was the first woman to win a Nobel Prize. She discovered the elements polonium and radium. These elements give off energy. The kind of energy they produce is called **radiation**. Curie made the first **X-ray** machine. An X-ray machine uses radiation to see inside objects, such as the human body.

3. EXPERIMENT

Create an experiment to help answer your question. Write down the steps. Make a list of the supplies you'll need. Then do the experiment. Write down what happens.

4. ANALYSIS

Study the results of your experiment. Did it answer your question? Was your guess correct?

5. CONCLUSION

Think about how the experiment went. Why was your guess wrong or right? Write down the reasons.

MATERIALS

Here are some of the materials that you will need for the experiments in this book.

 9-VOLT BATTERY

 BAKING SHEET

 BAKING SODA

 BOWL

 EGGS

 ELECTRICAL TAPE

 EPSOM SALT

 FOOD COLORING

 INSULATED WIRE

 MAGNETIC WAND

 MASON JAR WITH LID

 MEASURING CUPS & SPOONS

MUG

PAPER TOWELS

PASTA SERVER

PENCIL (#2)

PENCIL SHARPENER

PLASTIC ZIPPER BAGS

ROLLING PIN

RULER

SALT

SAND

SCISSORS

SPOON

THIN CARDBOARD

TIMER

TOTAL BREAKFAST CEREAL

VINEGAR

WATER

WIRE STRIPPER

COLOR-MELT
MAGIC

MATERIALS: round bowl, water, baking sheet, salt, timer, food coloring

Trucks put salt on icy roads in winter. Why? There are compounds at work! At 32 degrees Fahrenheit (0°C), water's **molecules** press close together. They form ice. Salt interrupts this process. The salt compound breaks into molecules of sodium and chloride. These molecules push the water molecules apart. This makes it harder for the water to freeze.

WHY IT WORKS

The food coloring would stay on top of the ice without the salt. But the salt makes it hard for the water to stay frozen. The salt creates cracks as the ice melts. The food coloring flows into the cracks. The ice is now a cool work of art!

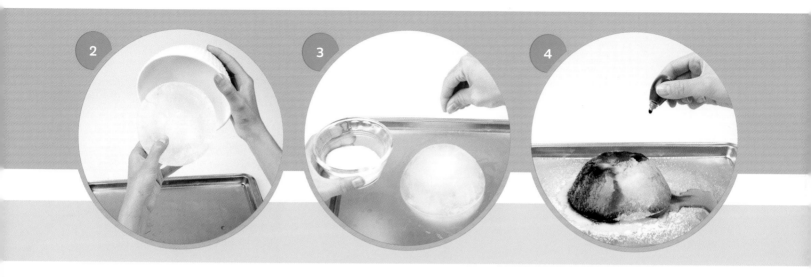

CREATE ART WITH COMPOUNDS!

① Fill the bowl with water. Leave it in the freezer overnight.

② Remove the ice from the bowl. Set it flat side down on the baking sheet.

③ Sprinkle salt on the ice. Wait 30 seconds.

④ Put drops of food coloring on the ice. Put the drops only on the top of the ice. Use different colors!

⑤ Watch what happens. The food coloring should spread throughout the ice!

COLORFUL
CRYSTALS

MATERIALS: measuring cups, Epsom salt, mug, hot water, food coloring, spoon, sand, bowl

A water **molecule** has two hydrogen atoms. Each has a positive **charge**. A water molecule has one oxygen atom. It has a negative charge. These two charges help the water molecule pull many other kinds of molecules toward it. The pull is strong. It can break down compounds such as sugar and salt.

GROW CRYSTALS WITH H$_2$O!

1. Pour ½ cup Epsom salt into a mug.

2. Measure ½ cup hot tap water. Mix in one drop of food coloring.

3. Add the colored water to the Epsom salt.

Continued on the next page.

COLORFUL CRYSTALS (CONTINUED)

4 Stir quickly for 2 minutes. Most of the salt should **dissolve**.

5 Drop one grain of sand into the mixture.

6 Put the mug in the freezer for 10 minutes. Then move it to the refrigerator. Leave it there for 24 hours.

7 Slowly pour out the extra liquid. This should reveal a colorful crystal garden!

8 Try the experiment with different colors!

WHY IT WORKS

Water **molecules** spread out when they are hot. This creates a lot of space for the Epsom salt to **dissolve**. But the freezer and the refrigerator cool the liquid. The water molecules press closer together. The Epsom salt is pushed out. Its molecules join together. They form their own solid structures. These are the beautiful crystals that we see!

RUBBER EGG

EGG

MATERIALS: raw egg,
mason jar with lid,
vinegar, pasta server

Acids and bases are compounds. They can **react** with each other. These reactions usually create water and salt.

WHY IT WORKS

Vinegar is an acid. An eggshell is a base made of calcium carbonate. The vinegar and the eggshell react with each other. The carbonate turns into carbon dioxide. It forms tiny bubbles on the egg. The bubbles of carbon dioxide **dissolve** the calcium, so the shell disappears. Then the vinegar hardens the egg. This makes the egg rubbery.

MAKE AN EGG BOUNCE!

① Put the egg in the jar. Add enough vinegar to cover the egg.

② Screw the lid onto the jar. Put the jar in the refrigerator for 24 hours.

③ Open the jar. Carefully scoop out the egg.

④ Dump out the vinegar. Return the egg to the jar. Cover it with fresh vinegar. Seal the jar. Refrigerate for another 24 hours.

⑤ Open the jar. Carefully scoop out the egg again. The shell should be gone!

⑥ Find an area that's easy to clean. Drop the egg and see what happens!

DOUBLE BUBBLE
PENCILS

MATERIALS: 2 pencils (#2), pencil sharpener, thin cardboard, scissors, glass jar, warm water, salt, spoon, ruler, 9-volt battery, electrical tape, 2 10-inch (25 cm) pieces of insulated wire, wire stripper

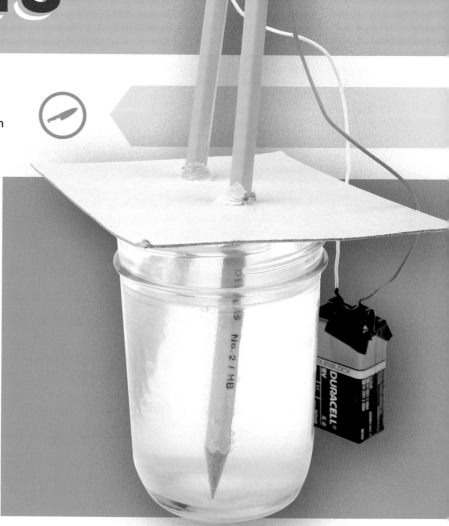

There are many ways to create a **reaction**. Electricity is one way to break down compounds. It can separate the atoms of a compound.

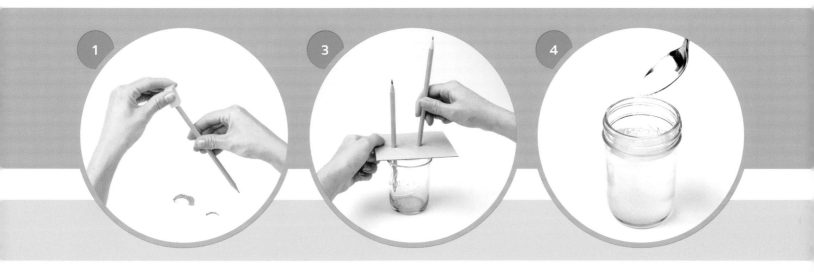

USE ELECTRICITY TO SPLIT WATER!

1 Pull the eraser and metal band off each pencil. Sharpen all four ends.

2 Trim the cardboard so it just covers the jar.

3 Stick the pencils through the cardboard. Make sure both pencils will fit inside the jar. Then set the cardboard and pencils aside.

4 Fill the jar with warm water. Add one spoonful of salt. Stir until the salt **dissolves**.

Continued on the next page.

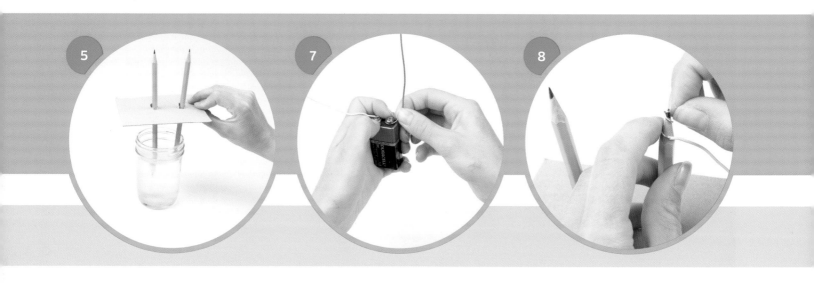

DOUBLE BUBBLE PENCILS (CONTINUED)

⑤ Place the pencils in the water. The cardboard should rest on the jar's rim.

⑥ Strip 1 inch (2.5 cm) of coating off both ends of each wire.

⑦ Wrap one end of each wire around each battery connector. Keep them in place with electrical tape.

⑧ Carefully wrap the other end of each wire around a pencil tip. The pencil tips in the water should begin to bubble!

Electricity travels from the battery through the wires, pencils, and salt water. Pencil lead is made of the metallic **mineral** graphite. It carries the electricity to the salt water. The electricity splits the water's **molecules**. The hydrogen and oxygen atoms are no longer bonded. This **reaction** creates the bubbles!

BAKING SODA BURST

MATERIALS: measuring spoons, baking soda, paper towel, measuring cups, water, vinegar, plastic zipper bag, food coloring

Not all **reactions** are the same. Some are slow and silent. Others are loud and sudden. Vinegar and baking soda react with each other. They create water and carbonic acid. But this acid immediately breaks down. It becomes carbon dioxide. That is a gas. Its bubbles can cause a foamy mess!

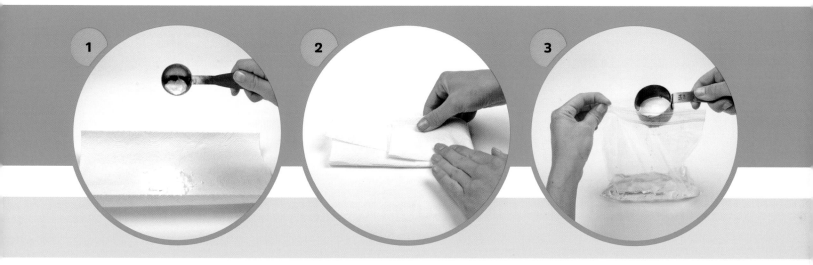

THIS REACTION ENDS WITH A BANG!

1 Put 1½ tablespoons of baking soda in the center of the paper towel.

2 Fold the paper towel around the baking soda. Make sure the baking soda can't fall out.

3 Put ½ cup of water and ¼ cup of vinegar in the plastic bag.

Continued on the next page.

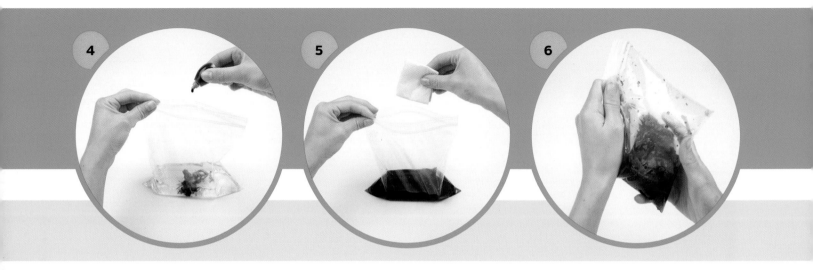

BAKING SODA BURST (CONTINUED)

4 Add a few drops of food coloring to the bag.

5 Find an area that's easy to clean. Put the paper towel in the bag and quickly seal it shut.

6 Shake the bag. Then gently set it down and wait. The bag should slowly swell until it bursts!

WHY IT WORKS

When the vinegar touches the baking soda, a **reaction** takes place. The vinegar and baking soda react to make carbon dioxide gas. The gas starts to fill the plastic bag. The pressure builds and builds. Then, *POP*!

ELEMENTAL
BREAKFAST

MATERIALS: Total® breakfast cereal, gallon plastic zipper bag, rolling pin, measuring cup, hot water, magnetic wand

Minerals are important parts of our daily diet. They help our bodies work properly. They also strengthen bones. Our bodies cannot make **minerals**. So, we must get them from the food we eat. Did you know minerals are also on the periodic table? **Zinc**, calcium, and iron are not just cereal ingredients. They are elements!

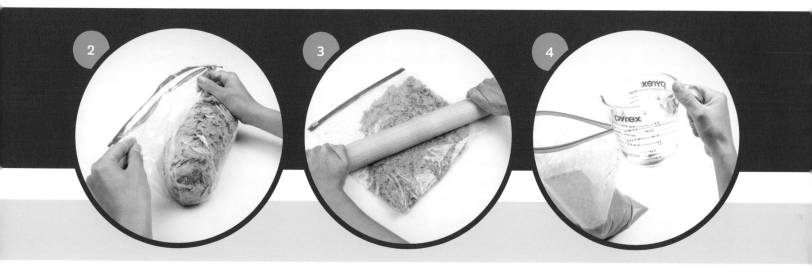

CAPTURE THE IRON IN YOUR DIET!

(1) Pour cereal into the plastic bag. Fill the bag almost all the way.

(2) Carefully press as much air out of the bag as you can. Seal it shut.

(3) Use the rolling pin to crush the cereal into powder. Add more cereal and crush again. Be sure not to make holes in the bag!

(4) Pour 12 cups of water into the bag. Seal it shut.

(5) Gently **squeeze** the bag to mix the water and cereal. Wait 15 minutes.

Continued on the next page.

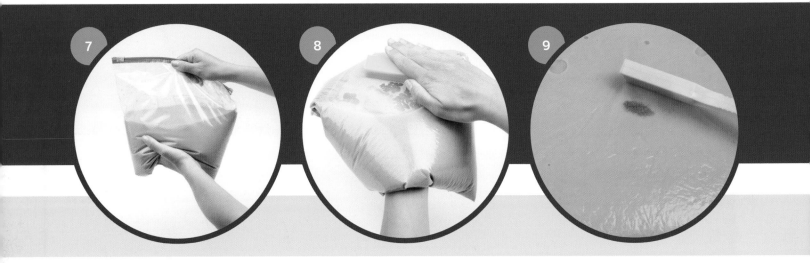

ELEMENTAL BREAKFAST (CONTINUED)

⑥ Repeat step 5 three more times.

⑦ Hold the magnet in your hand. Put the bag on top. Slowly move the bag in a circle on the magnet for 2 minutes.

⑧ Carefully turn the bag over. Keep the magnet in contact with the bag.

⑨ Slowly move the magnet around. You should see a dark clump following it. That's iron!

WHY IT WORKS

Iron is an important **mineral**. Iron in your blood carries oxygen throughout your body. Iron also makes your muscles strong. Tiny bits of iron are often added to cereal. The tiny iron bits stick to the dry cereal flakes. But crushing the cereal and adding water separates the iron from the cereal. Iron is magnetic, so it follows the magnet.

GLOSSARY

charge – a quantity of electricity. An electric charge is either positive or negative.

dissolve – to become part of a liquid.

mineral – a chemical element that occurs naturally in the ground.

molecule – a group of two or more atoms that make up the smallest piece of a substance.

radiation – a type of energy that forms waves.

react – to change when mixed with another chemical or substance.

research – the act of finding out more about something.

squeeze – to press the sides of something together.

starch – a white odorless tasteless substance that is found in plants such as potatoes and rice.

symbol – something that stands for something else.

X-ray – a type of energy that can go through solid objects.

zinc – a bluish-white metallic element.